# HISTORY'S MOST HAUNTED

# HAUNTED! THE TOWER OF LONDON

**Gareth Stevens**
Publishing

BY DREW NELSON

Please visit our website, www.garethstevens.com. For a free color catalog of all our high-quality books, call toll free 1-800-542-2595 or fax 1-877-542-2596.

**Library of Congress Cataloging-in-Publication Data**

Nelson, Drew.
Haunted! The tower of London / by Drew Nelson.
  p. cm. – (History's most haunted)
Includes index.
ISBN 978-1-4339-9264-3 (pbk.)
ISBN 978-1-4339-9265-0 (6-pack)
ISBN 978-1-4339-9263-6 (library binding)
1. Tower of London (London, England)—Juvenile literature. 2. London (England)—Buildings, structures, etc.—Juvenile literature. 3. Haunted places—Juvenile literature. 4. Ghosts—England—Juvenile literature. I. Nelson, Drew, 1986- II. Title.
BF1461.N45 2014
133.1—dc23

First Edition

Published in 2014 by
**Gareth Stevens Publishing**
111 East 14th Street, Suite 349
New York, NY 10003

Copyright © 2014 Gareth Stevens Publishing

Designer: Nicholas Domiano
Editor: Kristen Rajczak

Photo credits: Cover, p. 1 gagliardifoto/Shutterstock.com; p. 5 (map) Volina/Shutterstock.com; p. 5 (Tower of London) David Steele/Shutterstock.com, (Edinburgh Castle) Ross Strachan/Shutterstock.com; p. 6 Leemage/ Universal Images Group/Getty Images; pp. 7, 8 iStockphoto/Thinkstock.com; p. 9 Corel Professional Photos/ Wikimedia Commons; pp. 10, 13, 27 English School/The Bridgeman Art Library/Getty Images; p. 11 Rosakoalagliterzereinhorn/Wikimedia Commons; p. 12 David Williamson/Wikimedia Commons;
p. 15 photodisc/Thinkstock.com; p. 17 Google Art Project/Wikimedia Commons; p. 18 Cnyborg/Wikimedia Commons; p. 19 Edouard Cibot/The Bridgeman Art Library/Getty Images; p. 21 Mary Lane/Shutterstock.com;
p. 23 Universal Images Group/Universal Images Group/Getty Images; p. 25 DEA PICTURE LIBRARY/De Agostini Picture Library/Getty Images; p. 29 Photos.com/Thinkstock.com.

Printed in the United States of America

CPSIA compliance information: Batch #CS13GS: For further information contact Gareth Stevens, New York, New York at 1-800-542-2595.

# CONTENTS

Words in the glossary appear in **bold** type the first time they are used in the text.

# HAUNTING IN THE UNITED KINGDOM

There are spooky places all over the world. From the United States to China and everywhere in between, there are stories about ghosts and haunted buildings. A lot of stories about haunted places are told throughout the United Kingdom, which includes the countries of England, Northern Ireland, Scotland, and Wales.

There have been people living in the United Kingdom for thousands of years, so there are many very old places people think are creepy. Many wars and **revolutions** have been sources of scary, bloody stories. One of the most haunted places in the history of the United Kingdom is the Tower of London.

## THE HAUNTED KINGDOM

In Northern Ireland, there's a big home called Springhill that's said to house the ghost of a woman named Olivia. In Scotland, Edinburgh Castle has secret tunnels that have always been the subject of scary stories. In Wales, there are even stories about a ghost ship off the coast!

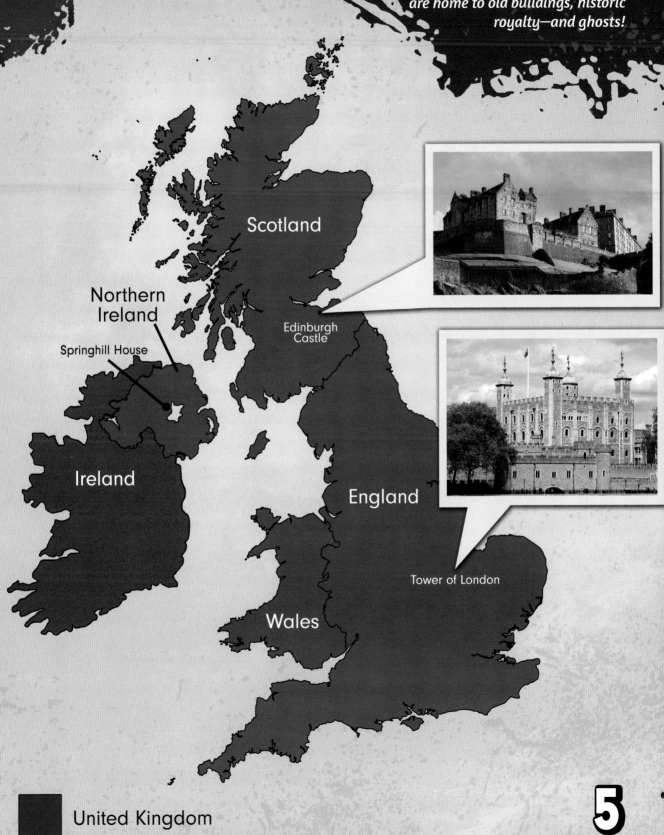

The countries in the United Kingdom are home to old buildings, historic royalty—and ghosts!

Scotland

Northern Ireland

Springhill House

Edinburgh Castle

Ireland

England

Wales

Tower of London

United Kingdom

# RAISING THE TOWER

Almost 1,000 years ago, a **Norman** ruler called William the Conqueror **invaded** England and made himself king. He took over the country's largest city, London. William knew he needed to protect himself from his enemies, and he ordered his army to build him a fortress, or a strong building somewhat like a castle.

**WILLIAM THE CONQUEROR**

They started work in the 1070s. By 1100, the White Tower was completed, but William had already died. This tower is still standing today at the center of the Tower of London.

## A LOOMING FIGURE

The White Tower was unlike anything ever seen in England before. It was huge, with four towers, one in each corner that could be seen from miles away. At its tallest point, the **stronghold** is 90 feet (27 m) tall. When it was built, giant Roman walls protected two sides.

The Tower of London is found on the north bank of the Thames River in the city of London.

# MEDIEVAL OR MEDI-EVIL?

During the **medieval** period, many different kings added to or improved parts of the Tower of London. The tower's oldest ghost stories come from around this time.

Henry III, a very young king, was building a new wall around the tower in 1238 when a ghost appeared and tore down a piece of it! Workers claimed it was

**KING HENRY III**

Thomas Becket, a saint in the Catholic Church who had been **executed** by Henry's grandfather. Henry immediately built a chapel and named it after Becket. This must have pleased the ghost, because the rest of the wall stayed put! By 1350, the tower looked mostly like it does today.

*This picture shows what the Tower of London looked like hundreds of years ago—and it's very similar to today!*

# THE BOY KING

Henry III became the king of England when he was only 9 years old. His father, John, had been fighting the French when he died, making the young Henry king of a country at war. One of the major acts of his rule was improving castles and fortresses around England, including the Tower of London.

# ROYAL REMAINS

For the next 200 years, each king who ruled over England oversaw the Tower of London. In 1471, the tower got its next famous ghost.

During the Wars of the Roses, many kings came and went quickly. When Henry VI was defeated, he was held in the Wakefield Tower in the Tower of London. Just before midnight on May 21, 1471, Henry was stabbed to death by the Duke of Gloucester.

**KING HENRY VI**

It's said that on the anniversary of his murder, Henry's ghost appears and paces around the Wakefield Tower until midnight. Then he fades back into the stones of the tower for another year.

## THE WARS OF THE ROSES

The Wars of the Roses were a series of battles between two families—the Yorks and the Lancasters. Both families were direct **descendants** of King Edward III and thought they should rule England. The conflicts were called the Wars of the Roses because the Yorks represented themselves with a white rose and the Lancasters used a red rose.

10

*Visitors to the Wakefield Tower, shown here, could meet the ghost of King Henry VI.*

# THE GHOSTLY PRINCES

More than 10 years later, after more fighting among the would-be kings, Edward IV died suddenly. His young son Edward was **heir** to the throne and was to become king of England. Parliament, the part of the British government that makes laws, said that neither Edward nor his younger brother had the right to become king.

**PRINCE EDWARD & PRINCE RICHARD**

Edward was 12 years old, and his brother, Richard, was 10 years old. They were sent to live in the Tower of London while their uncle, Richard III, was crowned. Their imprisonment didn't last long, however.

*Richard III was the Duke of Gloucester before becoming king. He was the same man who killed Henry VI in the Wakefield Tower!*

# NOT JUST A TOWER

The Tower of London has had many different uses in its long history. Some kings lived there. Starting in the early 1100s, it was used as a prison. Edward I used the tower to hold valuables. The Royal Mint, which prints money, was even housed in one part of the tower.

After a few months of living and playing inside the Tower of London, the two young princes suddenly vanished. They were never seen alive again. Most people believe they were murdered on the orders of Richard III, who was worried one of them would try to become king one day. While there's no proof of this, the skeletons of two young children were found hidden underneath a staircase in the White Tower in 1674.

Guards at the tower have said they've seen the ghosts of the two boys walking up and down that staircase hand in hand, wearing white nightshirts. Then they disappear once again.

## THE TOWER GREEN

Only certain people were executed inside the Tower of London on the Tower Green. They were either very important or had strong supporters who might cause problems at a public execution. Most of the executions took place on Tower Hill, a grassy hill just outside the tower's walls.

This beautiful fortress has a bloody, haunted past.

15

# A VIOLENT HUSBAND

One of the most well-known rulers in British history is King Henry VIII. He took over the Tower of London when he became king in 1509. He added more buildings to the tower, including wooden buildings within the walls for his wives.

Henry VIII had many wives. He kept taking new wives as he tried to find one who would give him a son to rule England after him. It was very important to Henry to keep the throne of England in his family. When his second wife, Anne Boleyn, had a daughter instead of a son, Henry was very angry.

## THE CHURCH OF ENGLAND

One of the reasons that Henry VIII wanted to have a male heir with a strong claim to the throne is because many people in England didn't approve of some of the things he was doing. For example, he split from the Catholic Church and created the Church of England, then made himself head of the church.

Henry VIII's children did sit on the throne of England. One of his daughters ruled as Queen Mary I. Another became Queen Elizabeth I.

Henry VIII had Anne Boleyn locked in the Tower of London. On May 19, 1536, he had her **beheaded** on Tower Green. Since then, Anne's ghost has been seen frequently in different places around the tower.

Her ghost is said to be seen on the green where she was executed. She has also been seen—sometimes headless— pacing around the Queen's House, a building that Henry had made for her inside the tower. There's even a story that many people have seen Anne Boleyn's ghost leading a procession through the Chapel Royal to the altar, under which her body is buried!

*Would you be afraid to look in the Queen's House and perhaps see Anne Boleyn's headless ghost?*

# GHOSTLY RERUNS

Anne Boleyn was just one of Henry VIII's wives executed at the Tower of London. Catherine Howard, the king's fifth wife, was beheaded there after less than 2 years of marriage. That's not the only thing the two women have in common, though. Anne Boleyn and Catherine Howard were cousins!

# THE HACKED COUNTESS

Anne Boleyn wasn't the only ghost that Henry VIII created in the Tower of London. The execution of Margaret Pole, Countess of Salisbury, is known as one of the bloodiest executions ever to take place at the tower.

The countess's son was a powerful man who opposed both the country's split from the Catholic Church and Henry's appointment of himself as the leader of the Church of England. He was in France, though, so Henry chose to punish his mother instead. He had the 72-year-old woman brought to the Tower of London to be executed on May 27, 1541.

## THE SALT TOWER

There's a very old section of the tower called the Salt Tower. It's said to be one of the most haunted places on the tower grounds. In 1864, a guard knocked himself out charging at a ghost there. Today, the Salt Tower has such a scary air that even dogs won't go in!

20

It was dangerous to oppose the king of England, especially when he'd already killed so many at the Tower of London.

**21**

When the countess was brought to the Tower Green, she refused to put her head down on the same block where others had been beheaded. The executioner swung his axe at her, but the countess started to run away. The executioner chased her down, swinging his axe, and eventually struck her enough times that she died in the yard.

Guards of the tower say that, every once in a while, on the anniversary of her death, her ghost reenacts the execution in the yard. The screaming countess runs away from her executioner, but it always ends the same way.

## GHOSTS DON'T HAVE TO BE HUMAN...

At one point, the Tower of London was the home of the Royal Menagerie, which housed lions, leopards, monkeys, bears, and even an elephant! One night in 1815, a guard claimed to see a bear roaming the halls. When he attacked it, he passed right through—the bear was a ghost!

Animals were kept at the
tower for about 600 years.

23

# THE 9 DAYS' QUEEN

Another famous female ghost of the Tower of London is Lady Jane Grey. When King Edward VI was dying, he named his cousin, Jane, as his **successor** rather than his sister, Mary. Jane became the queen and moved into the Tower of London.

After only 9 days, Jane was overthrown. At first, the new queen, Mary, set free both the 17-year-old Jane and her husband after a short imprisonment in the tower. However, both were eventually beheaded on the Tower Green.

The last time there was a report of Jane's ghost was on February 12, 1957. Two guards claimed to see her dressed all in white.

## 'TIL DEATH DO US PART

Visitors to the Tower of London have also seen the ghost of Lady Jane Grey's beheaded husband, Guildford Dudley. It's said that Dudley can be found crying in the Beauchamp Tower. No one knows why he's always so sad. Maybe it's because he was beheaded first!

After the guards saw Jane Grey's ghost in 1957, they realized it was the 403rd anniversary of her execution.

# A GHOSTLY RESIDENT

Another ghost of the Tower of London wasn't killed there but spent years imprisoned in its walls. Sir Walter Raleigh was first sent to the Tower of London after marrying a member of Queen Elizabeth's court without permission. He was only there for 2 months.

After Queen Elizabeth died, her successor, James I, claimed Sir Walter was plotting to overthrow him. For the next 13 years, Sir Walter lived in the Tower of London awaiting his death. He was let out briefly in 1616 to lead a voyage across the ocean. Against the king's order, he attacked a Spanish colony. When he returned, he was quickly beheaded.

## TWO FOR JAMES

James I may have been responsible for another tower ghost, too. Arbella Stuart, a possible successor to the throne, married a powerful man without James's permission. He arrested them both. Arbella tried to escape, but she was captured and brought to the Tower of London. She wouldn't eat and died in 1615 before her execution.

*Sir Walter is said to haunt the room he was imprisoned in for so many years, which can still be seen today.*

# THE MODERN TOWER

In the 1850s, the offices that had been housed at the Tower of London were removed, and old structures from medieval times were rebuilt.

The last execution at the Tower of London took place in 1941. The tower took bomb hits during **World War II**. These destroyed many buildings, though they have since been repaired. The last state prisoners were moved around this time, too.

While there aren't any more executions or prisoners at the Tower of London, the spirits of those who died there may yet remain. They haunt within the tower's walls to remind visitors of the bloody past.

## THE PEOPLE'S TOWER

Today, more than 2 million people from around the world visit the Tower of London each year. Visitors aren't new for the tower, though. There are records of people paying for guided tours dating all the way back to the 1590s. Half a million people were already visiting each year by 1901!

*The Tower of London is one of the most visited places in the United Kingdom.*

# GLOSSARY

**behead:** to kill someone by cutting off their head

**descendant:** a person who comes after another in a family

**execute:** to kill, often for doing wrong

**heir:** a person who will receive another person's property or rights after their death

**invade:** to enter a place to take it over

**medieval:** having to do with the Middle Ages, a time in European history from about 500 to 1500

**Norman:** a person from Normandy, France

**revolution:** a movement to overthrow an established government

**stronghold:** a place that has been strengthened, especially in case of an attack

**successor:** a person who comes after another in a position of power

**World War II:** a war fought from 1939 to 1945 that involved countries around the world

# FOR MORE INFORMATION

## BOOKS

Belanger, Jeff. *The World's Most Haunted Places.* New York, NY: Rosen Publishing, 2009.

Hynson, Colin. *The Tower of London.* Milwaukee, WI: World Almanac Library, 2005.

Riley, Gail Blasser. *Tower of London: England's Ghostly Castle.* New York, NY: Bearport Publishing, 2007.

## WEBSITES

### Haunted London–Tower of London Ghosts

*www.haunted-britain.com/Haunted_London.htm*
Check out this resource about the Tower of London and other supernatural locations all over the United Kingdom.

### Historic Royal Places

*www.hrp.org.uk/TowerOfLondon/*
Visit the official site of royal historic landmarks in England.

# INDEX